The Essential
Book of

EMPOWERMENT

For my daughter Hannah,
Who IS beautiful.
With all my love…

Whatever you can do or dream you can,
    begin it.
Boldness has genius, magic and power in it.
Begin it now.

GOETHE

Twenty years from now you will be more
disappointed by the things you didn't do
than by the ones you did. So throw off the
bowlines. Sail away from the safe harbour.
Catch the trade winds in your sails.
Explore. Dream. Discover.

MARK TWAIN

The Essential
Book of

EMPOWERMENT

GABRIELLE MANDER

First published in Great Britain in 2000 by
Michael O'Mara Books Limited
9 Lion Yard
Tremadoc Road
London SW4 7NQ

Copyright © 2000 Gabrielle Mander

A CIP catalogue record for this book is available from the British Library

ISBN 1-85479-512-0

1 3 5 7 9 10 8 6 4 2

Designed and typeset by Design 23

Printed in Great Britain by Cox and Wyman Limited,
Reading, Berks.

CONTENTS

INTRODUCTION

No bird soars too high if he soars with his own wings.

WILLIAM BLAKE

Empowerment – What a magnificent word! It sounds glorious doesn't it? Free, yet in control, strong, yet never forceful. I used to imagine that it was a gift that some tremendous power could offer to others from his or her munificence. Perhaps 'The Great and Magnificent Oz' could supply that missing mental agility, or tenderness, or courage that would make all the difference to one's life. You hear people say, 'He made it possible,' or 'She was the wind beneath my wings,' 'Behind every great man is a great woman,' 'The power behind the throne' and so on. But if most of us waited for someone else to puff up enough of a breeze to grant us the power to fly solo, we would remain rooted to the spot. Personal empowerment is not about asking someone to change your life, or waiting patiently for someone else to give you permission to let good things happen to you. Empowerment is about using *your* mind and imagination, *your* energy and *your* will to realise *your* dreams, to fulfil *your* boundless potential; to increase *your* success; to improve *your* health and to be happy and in control of *your* life.

Nowadays we talk of enabling people. Courageous and strong people with physical or mental disabilities concentrate their energy on what they *can* do and discourage others from emphasizing what they cannot. This is not just political correctness. All too often, we are hampered by conditioning or unhappy experience into recognizing only our limitations and not our potential. In recent years we have discovered what a difference words can make to our perceptions. We define the differences between those who can see and those who cannot, or those who can hear and those who cannot, by referring not to the blind and the deaf, but to the sighted and to the hearing. We do not concentrate on the disabling aspects of society and this frees us to re-examine our ideas and our prejudices.

The emphasis in this book is on the power of words. I first began to think about this after reading a splendid and beautifully written piece in the *Guardian* newspaper by Judith Williamson. It was written as Mr Tony

Blair's New Labour government came to power in Britain. Ms Williamson was examining the way New Labour had redefined its policies and manifesto to win the General Election. She referred in particular to the word 'socialism', which they had eliminated from their political vocabulary. This was a word that had been at the very heart of the Labour Party's political beliefs. She predicted that this word and all it meant would disappear from mainstream British politics within a very short space of time, and indeed, two years later it has. Whatever one's feelings about this particular issue, the principle serves to make a point. The words we use to express ideas have great power, and the perceptions of a nation, if not the world, can be shifted completely in two short years by changing them.

When I began the research for this book, I was sceptical about a form of self-hypnosis and re-education that would be as effective as New Labour 'spin doctoring'. And yet, have you noticed how quickly catch phrases from popular television shows or advertising campaigns enter the national vocabulary? I also recollect that the first words of *The Book of Genesis* in the Christian Bible are 'In the beginning was the word, and the word was God and the word was with God.' I have read many books and articles on the subject of affirmations and empowerment and some are written from a position of deeply held faith or conviction, or a belief in divine inspiration. Others are motivated by the 'success now' principle. I have tried to bear all these concepts in mind and I have tried some of the ideas suggested here myself. I am still learning to be self-disciplined and like most of us, I find it difficult to devote enough time and consistent effort to have changed my life completely. However I did try a programme of very simple one-word affirmations – 'Open' 'Focus' and 'Energy' – to see if it would help me to concentrate and devote the time needed to write this book. I was also working at a challenging, full-time job and balancing the joys of, and my obligations to, my family and friends. And here it is.

NEW TRICKS AND LEOPARD'S SPOTS

Watch your thoughts; they
become your words.
Watch your words; they
become your actions.
Watch your actions; they
become your habits.
Watch your habits; they
become your character.
Watch your character for it
will become your destiny.

THE POWER TO CHANGE

If we are unhappy about the way our lives are going, we sometimes look outside ourselves for help to make important changes. Spirituality in whatever form or denomination can enrich our lives immeasurably. The right professional advice on career changes, health or personal fitness can be hugely beneficial when we know the direction in which we want to move. *Never* underestimate the value of generosity of spirit, love and support wherever you meet it. But too many of us expect very little from life and of ourselves and most of us fail to recognize a challenge as an opportunity. Personal empowerment is the ability to change that forever.

Some people have spent a lifetime believing that their dreams will never come true; that their hard work will probably go unacknowledged; that their voices will never be heard above the roar of the crowd shouting its hopes and dreams into the ether. Some people are not obviously academic at school; most of us are told that it is boastful and unattractive to proclaim our achievements. During childhood and adolescence we are socialized, trained to live and work together and we are often given mixed messages. 'Pride comes before a fall' – 'Do not hide your light under a bushel;' 'Look before you leap;' – 'He who dares wins;' 'I want never gets.' – 'If you don't ask you don't get,' and so on and so on… Confusing isn't it?

In contrast, the precepts of personal empowerment are very straightforward. Words have influenced your personal growth and development and different words repeated frequently, in a positive way, with emotional intensity can make your intangible thoughts and dreams manifest in your life.

You and you alone *can* change the habits of a lifetime. 'You *can* teach an old dog new tricks'. 'A leopard *can* change its spots'.

Most of us *think* that there is something wrong with some aspect of our bodies, our sex-lives, our relationships or our work. Our *thoughts* become our *words*, our words our *actions* and our actions our habits. We think we are unattractive and we fail to smile. We

think we are unlovable and we send
that message to those we wish would
love us. We expect to be overlooked for
promotion and we are not
disappointed. A friend of mine once
told me that we get what we expect,
not what we deserve. Sadly, he was
right. But habits can be changed and
the destiny we deserve is within the
control of each and every one of us:
'Ding Dong the witch is dead' – you do
not have to wait to be discovered! You
do not have to espouse a cult
philosophy; you just have to take
responsibility for the changes you want
to make.
No one can do it for you.

Empowerment comes from identifying
what you want to achieve, accepting

that you can only change yourself, and harnessing the tremendous reserves of unused potential that you possess, to make your dreams come true. It's as simple as that, but that doesn't mean that it's easy. It takes time and it requires perseverance, determination and practice, but above all it demands that crucial step, accepting that change is possible.

The techniques to use in the coup d'état you are about to achieve in taking back your power are many. Some books suggest that unravelling the messages of your unconscious mind, and working on the lessons learned can be a good start. Relaxation, meditation, yoga, stress and anger management, dream analysis, visualisation and the main topic of this book affirmations, have all been found to be extremely successful in effecting tremendous changes for the good.

Please remember however, if you feel that you have a serious problem with substance or alcohol abuse, depression, eating disorders or alienation it is important to seek professional help and guidance. Therapy, analysis or medical treatment can be extremely beneficial and, in these circumstances, your doctor should be your first port of call. That being said, many people who simply feel disempowered by circumstances and their life experiences can benefit from a programme of self-help or complementary therapy. Before you take on the challenges of throwing off old habits and conditioning however, it is a good idea to address some of the major obstacles that we in the 21st century have placed in our own paths.

Most of us suffer from stress and from the pressures of earning a living, raising families and keeping pace with the enormous acceleration of changes in our working practices, technology and the environment. We often feel powerless in the face of these obstacles. It is true we can use our democratic rights, our intelligence and our integrity to influence the wider world, but the most immediate and effective change we can make is in our own personal responses to change and to stress. We need to relax, eat well, sleep well and take regular exercise. 'Easier said than done' I hear you say!

It is quite likely that you are already working on establishing a healthy diet, taking light exercise and trying to get plenty of rest. It is less likely that you have given yourself a break and really addressed coping with stress and learning to relax. You may be sceptical about the benefits of real relaxation, but no one can tackle a programme of self-education with an exhausted body and a mind in turmoil. This is not a luxury, it's a necessity – and only by relaxing completely are you likely to succeed. There are several ways in which it is possible to prepare yourself for a life-changing experience. Think of this as warming up for your intensive intellectual and emotional workout.

RELAXATION
Mastering true relaxation is a skill and like any skill, learning to play the piano, laying bricks or surfing the net, it takes practice. It has been suggested that the state of deep relaxation, which can be achieved with a few simple techniques, is as beneficial as five or six hours of deep, recuperative sleep. The amount of energy you burn up can decrease dramatically. The amount of blood that passes through the heart – or cardiac output – also falls significantly when you are in a state of deep relaxation. Everyone finds his or her own ideal way to relax. For some it

is sitting comfortably, listening to music. For others, dancing the night away is what it takes to recharge their batteries. Swimming, reading, a work-out at the gym, cycling, walking or enjoying a meal with friends or family; it doesn't really matter which you choose, as long as you relax completely, and forget the cares of the day.

Most of us will recognize that one or more of the above may represent a brief holiday from tension and anxiety.
I learned to tap dance in my mid-thirties. I am sure that I looked ridiculous, but I felt marvellous! The combination of the concentration required to master the steps; the thrilling soundtracks to which we danced; and the buzz I got out of

making percussive music with my feet meant that I forgot all the cares of motherhood and work for one blissful hour a week. I found that I felt more positive and creative on my way home after a class than in the eight hours that I sat in front of my computer – and I slept well too! I had a brief flirtation with sailing and an even briefer fling (literally) with skiing, and both combined concentration (in my case to survive), with an enforced distance from my everyday world, telephones and problems.Very relaxing!

But enough about me. I mention this only to illustrate that anything which works for you is good. Please don't be alarmed, there are other ways to relieve tension and stress which don't involve fishnet tights, salopettes, the Jolly Roger or a top hat!

MEDITATION
Meditation is a very useful aid to relaxation and is a technique that will enhance the effectiveness of the visualisation and affirmation exercises that are central to empowerment. I am sure that you are aware that it has been practised for centuries in eastern culture, and forms a central part of many religious practices such as Islamic sufi, Chinese tao and Japanese zen. Incidentally, it has a vital part to play in Christian practice too. Many doctors in the west have also come to value its beneficial effects in recent years, as a non-pharmaceutical treatment for stress and anxiety. On a physical level it has

been found to reduce body temperature and lower blood pressure whilst increasing oxygen and lowering the heart rate. On a psychological level its practitioners benefit enormously from simply choosing to set aside a peaceful time for themselves. In the context of personal empowerment, this is a very important issue. *Make time for yourself!* The clarity of mind and heightened sense of awareness that is experienced in a meditative state is also most conducive to the exercises and techniques you will be mastering.

MEDITATION TECHNIQUES

There are many meditation techniques, and a good book or evening class will teach them. But it is important to stress that there is no right or wrong way to do it. It is a state of being, not a competitive sport and every experience is unique. You may try several techniques before you find one that suits you. The aim is to empty your mind, by concentrating on one single thing to the exclusion of all else. It might be a word, or a picture, or a sound, but together with a conducive atmosphere, a warm and comfortable position and deep breathing, meditation should result in a state of deep relaxation combined with a simultaneous clarity of mind. To be successful you need to practise meditation regularly for about ten to twenty minutes, twice a day.

BREATHING MEDITATION
This is probably the simplest method of all. We all know how to breathe. The secret of meditative breathing is to breathe properly, and to use the rhythm of breathing in and out to concentrate your mind, to become one with the natural rhythm of life, as it were. This sounds rather airy-fairy and esoteric, though actually it's completely straightforward. It's simple.
Breathe normally through your nose, mouth gently closed. Focus your mind on the sound and feel of your breath, as your abdomen rises and falls. Follow the rhythm of your breath with your

thoughts. If you are distracted by other notions as you do this, don't worry – simply allow them to drift in and out of your head and try to bring your focus back to your breath. Don't force yourself to concentrate – simply let it happen. Eventually, meditation will become as easy as falling asleep. When your time is up, take a deep breath, open your eyes, stretch and return to your normal state slowly and gently.

All you are trying to do is teach your conscious mind to concentrate on one thing. When you have mastered this, you might want to move on to a more advanced yogic breathing technique. The best position in which to do this is lying on your back on the floor, or on a firm mattress. Place one hand on your stomach so that you can feel the movement of air in and out of your body as you breathe. Before you start, exhale any stale air from your lungs, pushing it out through your nose until your lungs are completely empty. Now, the breath is divided into three parts: inhalation, retention and exhalation. Breathe in for a count of one, when you will feel your stomach expand; then hold your breath for a count of four; and exhale slowly for a count of two, allowing your stomach to contract again as you empty your lungs. As this becomes easier, the relaxation and the meditation will become more intense.

❧

THE CANDLE FLAME

Have you ever noticed that when you turn the light out, before you go to sleep, you carry an imprint of the light, in the sudden darkness, if only for a few seconds? Well, imagine holding that image of concentrated light for minutes, though the image will be less harsh. Light a candle in a darkened room. If you feel that a scented candle is conducive to relaxation, try lavender – and sit comfortably with your back straight and your shoulders relaxed. The tip of your nose should be in line with your navel. If you can place the candle at eye-level it will be easier. Fold your hands softly in your lap and breathe deeply as suggested above. Close your eyes and compose your mind. After a minute or so, open your eyes and look at the candle flame; keep breathing and concentrate all your thoughts on the image in front of you. Don't worry if you get distracted, just gently bring your thoughts and your gaze back to the flame. After about five minutes, close your eyes again. You should be able to hold the image of the flame in your mind's eye, just as you saw it a moment before. Keep breathing and concentrating for about ten to fifteen minutes. If the image fades, open your eyes and re-focus on the real flame. Now close your eyes again. Believe me, it gets easier. This same technique can be used looking at the sky, or an object like a flower or indeed a crystal. If you are aware of and feel convinced by the power of crystals, holding one while you meditate can be very effective.

TRANSCENDENTAL MEDITATION

Remember all that sitar music and The Beatles tearing off to India to listen to the wisdom of the Maharishi? Transcendental meditation became very popular in the early 1970s. In fact it is not so different from the techniques described above, except that it is based on a special word or phrase, known as a mantra, which you repeat to yourself silently, time and time again. A mantra is a completely meaningless word that is unlikely to distract you from what you are doing. I tried this with *haloumi* (a Greek cheese) because I liked the sound of the word and it worked perfectly well. The important thing is that you should not attach any emotional value to the word. As you sit or lie comfortably in a quiet room, breathe deeply and repeat your mantra to yourself. Your mind will become empty, and eventually, you will find it impossible to think of anything else. Once again, if you get distracted – don't worry, it just takes practice, don't give up – simply start repeating your mantra to yourself again and have another go. Remain passive, and maintain a relaxed attitude towards any distractions. You are relieving your stress, so worrying about being unable to maintain concentration will not help.

To sum up, the aim of relaxation and learning to induce a meditative state is to ease stress and leave your mind clear and focused. Then you can begin to offer your subconscious some new ideas to work upon – ideas about your self-worth, your hopes and dreams, and eventually, to make those hopes and dreams a reality.

DREAM, DREAM, DREAM

Your vision will become
clear only when you look
into your heart.
Who looks outside, dreams.
Who looks inside awakens.

CARL GUSTAV JUNG

DREAM WORKING

Dreaming is an extraordinary thing. We all do it, and to be deprived of the REM sleep we need for dreaming can result in severe mental trauma and disorientation. Sometimes our dreams are commonplace – a re-run of our day, with all its nuances and impressions. But at other times our dreams are more important. They may be the free movies that our subconscious runs for us, in an attempt to remind our conscious minds of something we need to know. Therapists use dream analysis as a way of helping their clients to recognize hidden fears and neuroses, hopes and disappointments.

In the quest for personal empowerment, dreams can provide useful clues to the subconscious conditioning we all experience throughout our lives. Understanding your dreams can help you to recognize and deal with negative feelings or lack of confidence which may be holding you back. Also, a basic understanding of the symbolism of dreams can help us to cope with the anxiety that so-called 'bad dreams' can cause. Dream symbolism is a vast subject and many volumes have been written, from academic theses to popular dictionaries of dream symbols. In this book I have only enough space to introduce you to the concept of attempting to use an interpretation of your dreams to identify areas of your life which may need a little work. Some people have found dream analysis invaluable in freeing them from anxiety about some aspects of their personalities. They are able to move on, using their knowledge to eliminate negative feelings about themselves.

Many people find that keeping a diary of their dreams helps them to understand more about their unconscious fears and desires. Others claim to have mastered the art of 'lucid dreaming', that is directing and controlling their dreams. Still others use affirmations to incubate dreams; that is to ask their subconscious to provide the answers to specific questions. Meditation, visualisation and affirmation can be handy tools in preparing the conscious mind to remember your dreams on waking. If you find dream working appealing, I recommend buying a good book devoted to the subject. However, some simple techniques follow to help you remember and analyse your dreams and I offer an example of the technique of interpretation in practice to whet your appetite.

REMEMBERING YOUR DREAMS

It is infuriating isn't it, to wake from a fascinating dream, with the secret of the universe on the tip of your tongue, only to drift off to sleep five minutes later and deprive mankind of your wisdom forever? No trick for remembering your dreams will be one hundred percent successful, but one or all of the following might help.

1 Before you go to sleep, do a simple breathing exercise to induce a state of relaxation, and try to empty your mind and focus on your breathing. Compose a simple, single sentence like 'On waking, I will remember my dreams, clearly and distinctly.' Repeat this to yourself firmly, at least ten times. Try to hold this thought as you are dropping off to sleep. Do not get too downhearted if you do not succeed immediately. You will need two things to make this technique work: practice and a positive belief that it will work, and even the latter will take practice!

2 Place something beside your bed that would not normally be there. Try a stone, a crystal, or even a cuddly toy. The aim is to identify this alien object

with remembering your dream.
Concentrate on it before you go to
sleep and tell yourself that when you
wake up and see it, you will recall your
dream.

3 As soon as you remember your
dream, write it down. Even this is
easier said than done – you will
probably wake at two o'clock in the
morning with your mind full of a
dream, but be unable to struggle to
consciousness in order to pick up a
pen. You may have to force yourself to
do it the first few times, but it soon
becomes an automatic response, and
you will be able to go back to sleep
without difficulty. Even then, you might
find that your nocturnal scrawl makes
absolutely no sense the following

morning. Don't be discouraged, it will get easier.

4 You could shake your partner awake and insist that he or she listen to you recount every detail, but this is not recommended as being conducive to a happy and lasting relationship. If you sleep alone you can use a tape recorder, to describe your dream, but most people find a pen and paper the most civilized solution. To begin with, just write down the salient points and try to fill in the details later.

The next stage is to try to interpret your dreams and see what significance, if any, they hold. Remember that we all have lots of dreams that are just a way of sorting and ordering our daily experiences. If you use a dictionary of dream symbols it is also important to remember that some people, places and objects will have a particular significance for you, which will not appear in any dictionary of symbols. Dream working is not an exact science, but it can act like a decoder to unravel the messages that our unconscious minds are trying to send.

INCUBATING DREAMS AND LUCID DREAMING

Many people believe that if you can master the art of remembering and decoding your dreams you can begin to direct them and use them to discover the answers to vital questions. Let us imagine that you feel vaguely uneasy about the progress of a friendship. Before you go to sleep, concentrate on clearing and focusing your mind. Formulate a question in such a way that the answer cannot be confusing. For example in the hypothetical situation above, do not ask 'Why do I feel uneasy?' The answer might be that you have exceeded your credit card limit or that your job is not fulfilling. You must frame your question in such a way that it is unequivocal, for example, 'Why do my encounters with X leave me with a feeling of unease?' The theory is that if you ask this question firmly and with intensity before you go to sleep, repeating it several times, the analysis of the dreams that follow could provide an answer to your confused feelings.

It has been suggested that it is a good idea to invent a small ritual to reinforce the message to your subconscious. Light a scented candle, or hold a crystal whilst you repeat the question. It is essential that you believe that it is possible to achieve the desired effect if this technique is to work.

Now you must tell yourself that you will remember your dream when you wake up and hope that you understand the answer. It may not be obvious on first analysis. It may also take some time for the message to be answered at all. Please remember too that it is your own feelings which will become clearer using this technique. It is not fortune-telling. Never act on the apparent answer to an incubated dream if you feel truly uncomfortable with the answer. Do not expect overnight success either. It may take several attempts before any answer becomes clear. If you can master this skill your sleeping and waking hours could become a great deal richer and more interesting.

Lucid dreaming is an even more advanced technique, in which the dreamer becomes able to condition his or her subconscious to allow him to be aware that he is dreaming and direct the action of his dream. Once again this involves establishing a ritual and affirming your intention with conviction before sleeping. In this instance you might plant a code in your unconscious, such as a colour or a number which will indicate that you are dreaming. This is quite an advanced technique which I recommend you study in more detail before attempting it. To conclude this chapter I would like to give an example of a dream and its analysis to illustrate how this technique can increase understanding and relieve anxiety, leaving the dreamer empowered to follow a course that leads to greater happiness.

Sally is a seventeen-year-old in her final year at school. She was very distressed to have a dream that, she imagined, showed that she wished the entire year below her at school to be massacred by machine-gun fire. During the bloodbath, she enjoyed a wonderful party at her father's beautiful house in the South of France, with her dearest friends and family around her. Sally was horrified to imagine that she harboured violent and destructive impulses towards her schoolfellows and seemed just to party on as they perished.

However, when she told a friend about this dream, the friend was able to offer the following interpretation.

Firstly, the friend suggested, other people in our dreams often represent other aspects of ourselves, and houses too are considered to represent different aspects of our own personalities. The destruction of the children in the year below was an acknowledgement that Sally was growing up; she would be leaving school that year, and that her younger self she felt, would no longer exist. These younger children represented the elimination of all that was to follow, when she no longer attended school. This could be an expression of her sadness that this part of her life was over. It was hard for her to imagine that school with all its routines and joys would simply carry on when she was no longer part of it. Symbolically, Sally dealt with this regret by wiping out both her younger self and the potential for school to continue without her. In part, Sally was delighted to be moving on to new and exciting things, and the terrific party in the wonderful and glamorous house represented this. This house actually existed and was very special to Sally, but it also represented the grown-up world she hoped waited for her in the future. In her dream, her father tried to help her schoolmates and survived the onslaught of bullets. Sally was very close to her father and recognized in her dream that he had helped her through painful adolescence and would also be there in her grown-up future. Considered in this light, Sally's nightmare becomes a healthy and positive resolution of her hopes and fears in a period of great change, full of both excitement and sadness. Sally was able to see this and she was no longer afraid that she had secret violent urges. She left school and became a successful artist and a happy and thoughtful adult.

ACCENTUATE
THE
POSITIVE

I have learned, that if one advances confidently in the direction of his dreams, and endeavours to live the life he has imagined, he will meet with a success unexpected in common hours.

HENRY DAVID THOREAU

VISUALISATION

Visualisation, like dream working, is another vast subject; indeed one of the books in this series deals with it in great detail. Although I can only touch on it here, it can be very effective in regaining your personal power. Visualisation is using the power of your imagination to create an image which though not 'real', in the sense that it is not three-dimensional and physical, it can nonetheless be seen, heard, touched, tasted and smelt, even inhabited in your mind's eye at will. If you have ever daydreamed about lying on a warm tropical beach, the water lapping at your feet and the sun warming your skin; or counted those dreary sheep over the stile to help you sleep, then you have experienced visualisation, at least passively. Do you remember as a small child, how you could become completely absorbed in a game of imagination? Perhaps you were a princess or a pirate, Robin Hood or a small, furry woodland creature. The point is that you could enter into the game and be whatever you wanted to be.

I remember playing a game as a small child, which I called 'runaway princesses'. I would start by closing my eyes and imagining what I looked like. I was tall, with raven hair and flashing violet eyes. I was dressed in silver silk with jewels in my hair and I was running away on a chestnut mare. Then I would enter into a full-length feature film in my imagination. I cannot now remember what I was running away from, but I always triumphed, even when I was a small, elfin redhead, dressed in the softest emerald-green suede. I suppose the nearest modern equivalent to visualisation is computer-generated 'virtual reality'. The advantage of visualisation is that you can do it anywhere and it has no adverse effects on your telephone bill.

ACTIVE VISUALISATION

The aim here is to practise, just as you have your relaxation techniques, till you have trained your imagination to follow your will.

Set aside an extra ten minutes after your relaxation or meditation exercises to practise visualisation. Start with simple exercises and do not be discouraged if you cannot hold images for very long to begin with.

First, do a deep-breathing exercise to slow your heart rate and put you in a receptive state. Then try the simplest of meditation exercises, the candle exercise is a good one to clear and focus your mind. Now concentrate on a familiar or favourite object. An article of clothing can be an interesting starting point. For example, I have a favourite jumper and when I first started to try visualisation, I used it for practice.

I would take my jumper from its drawer and lay it on the bed in front of me. I would unfold it and hold it to my face to breathe in the scent of freshly-washed wool and fabric softener. I would feel its texture between my fingers and look at the lovely, emerald-green colour. (No, I am not an elfin redhead!) Then I would pull it over my head, feeling the shape and texture against my skin. I would take it off, fold it up and put in back in the drawer. Next I would sit in my chair comfortably and breathe deeply for a minute or two, to clear and focus my mind. Then I would go through the whole process in my mind's eye. I would try to see the jumper, smell its scent, feel its texture and try to summon up as many details about it as I could. Finally, I would open my eyes, take the jumper from the drawer and see how close I had come in my visualisation to the real experience.

You can try this with much simpler

objects, a pen or a coffee cup for example. The point is to practise until your virtual experience is as close as possible to the reality. When you have mastered simple exercises, move on to something a little more complex. Take a short walk down your street, or in the garden, for example. Pay very close attention to every nuance of the experience because you will be trying to recall as many details as possible. When you return sit down, breathe deeply and try to relive the trip in your mind's eye. Start with getting up from your chair, opening the door, the feel of the door knob beneath your hand, the way the air changed as you went from indoors to out. The sounds that you heard; birds singing, a dog barking in the distance, a car starting up, the drone of a bus changing gear, people shouting, the sound of your own footsteps. Don't make the walk too long to start with. The important thing is to be able to recall the very texture of the experience. Incidentally, there are unexpected benefits from this technique. You will find that your powers of observation and of recall will improve quite dramatically, and your enjoyment of quite simple pleasures in life, like the smell of fresh coffee or the feel of the warmth of the sun on your head, are impossible not to experience with more intensity. (This may even result in new career opportunities as a private eye.)

After a while, you will be able to embroider your visualisations, adding a little something of your own imagining to the experience. Perhaps you will meet an old friend, or make a new one, or scented flowers will be growing in your garden as you pass. In time you will become so proficient that you can make this short journey anytime you choose. The next stage is to learn how to visualise a special place. It can be anywhere, a room or a garden, a beach or in the countryside, but it will be a place where you are in control, of the light, the temperature, the sounds and the sights, and it will be a place where you can feel truly happy and at peace. With practice this will become a place to which you can go anytime that you like to take a little time to restore your spirits. This can be a fantastic way to relieve stress. Take a deep breath and take yourself away for a blissful break.

I distrust instinctively statements such as 'Even a child of three could do it.' Such remarks only make me feel inadequate, which is just what we want to avoid, but small children do suffer from stress. At the very least, the following personal experience might be useful to the exhausted parents of active toddlers, and it does illustrate the effectiveness of visualisation, even in its simplest form.

 When my daughter was little and had just started at nursery school, all her new experiences made her overexcited and sometimes anxious and unable to sleep. When I invented 'the worry sack', and later 'floating down the river', I had never heard of visualisation, but these imaginary games worked like magic.

She would think about the things that were worrying her as she lay in bed, after a warm bath and several stories (or the same story, several times!). Sometimes she would tell me about her cares and sometimes she couldn't find the words. But I would sit beside her and hold open a large, imaginary sack. When she was ready, she would put the worries into the sack one-by-one. Sometimes she described them as wriggling or fighting back. When she had finished, I would tie the sack and struggle across the room, buckling under its weight. I would open her bedroom window and untying it carefully, shake the sack into the evening air. As her worries flew out of the window they became light and floated into the sky and away. We would cuddle for a while, and a song or story later, she would be peacefully asleep.

As she got older she found it helpful if she closed her eyes, and I described a scene in what I fondly thought of as a sonorous voice. She, our two cats and myself would be lying comfortably in a boat, floating gently down a sunny stream. The boat would nudge the banks of the river from time-to-time, the warm sun was on her face and birds were singing sweetly in the distance. She would be trailing her fingers in the water, which was cool and clear. As she did so all her cares would flow out of her fingertips and into the water, where they would be carried over a waterfall and out eventually, to the sea. The boat would turn calmly towards the bank and come to rest, bobbing softly by the bank and she would fall asleep with the sunshine on her face. Invariably she would fall asleep immediately the boat came to rest. She is now eighteen and in the midst of exams, and she still floats down the river occasionally. She can go to that place at will and feel safe and peaceful.

That is your aim.

These are examples of very simple visualisations, which nonetheless work to relieve anxiety and stress. *The Essential Book of Visualisation* offers many more and also goes into the many benefits of this technique in managing pain, conquering addictions, handling anger and its use in complementary medicine. Here we are concerned with visualisation as an aid to positive thinking and taking control of your life. Even these simple exercises, in conjunction with the relaxation and yoga techniques, will set you well on the way to controlling and overcoming some of the obstacles which stand between you and the self you deserve to be.

Here is one further example that might illustrate this point.

Annabel is a very successful businesswoman, working in a very high-powered job for one of the world's largest international banks.

She is an American working in England and she found that her American education and no-nonsense approach to getting results sometimes created difficulties with her male colleagues and superiors. Some cynics might think they were envious of her success as an attractive and intelligent woman. Her bank had a series of compulsory appraisals and Annabel found that her male boss would frequently downgrade her as 'too assertive'. Annabel was bewildered and hurt by these assessments and was afraid that she would get angry, so she began underachieving to ingratiate herself with the assessor. Sadly, this resulted in his downgrading her for under-achievement and for being too passive. She became anxious and depressed.

The prospect of the appraisals became a torment and she began to have panic attacks. Then a friend taught her some very simple exercises.

Firstly, Annabel needed practical first aid to control the stress and anxiety. A simple visualisation in which she watched a heavy pendulum swing back and forth, helped to slow her breathing and control the panic attacks. Then she needed to understand that she was unlikely to be able to change her superior's attitude and perceptions. She could however change her response to them. It was within her power to refuse to believe his biased opinion of her; after all she knew that she was an accomplished, experienced, negotiator. Together she and her friend created a virtual 'anger room', to which Annabel could retreat and express her fury at the unfairness, as she saw it, of the situation in which she found herself. With practice, these visualisations became the work of moments when she needed them. Then in the coming months, they worked on a complex visualisation to overcome the one area of Annabel's professional life in which she repeatedly underachieved and that gave her boss his ammunition. An important aspect of her job was to present and sell complex, computer-business solutions to very high-powered bankers at conferences all over the world. Annabel loathed this part of her job. Despite being exceptionally well-prepared and best qualified for the job, as she was very diligent, intelligent, articulate and attractive, she became frozen with anxiety as she got up to speak.

The first task she and her friend undertook was to examine her many great gifts and qualities, as honestly as she could and to acknowledge them. Together they wrote them down in a small but exquisite, handmade, paper notebook. Much of the description of Annabel that I have given here was included as a series of affirmations: I am in control. I am well-prepared. I am attractive. I am well-liked. I am expert at my job, etc. etc. Then they created a visualisation in which all these qualities were packed into a very smart suitcase and Annabel with her real luggage carried this case when she travelled to the conferences. The night before a presentation, when she was confident that all the equipment was working, had revised her notes and checked out the conference room, she would choose her outfit for the presentation and have a warm relaxing bath, with aromatherapy oil. She would get into bed and do some breathing exercises to relax. Then she would use the following visualisation, which was also written down, in her notebook.

She would go to the wardrobe and take down the imaginary suitcase, place it on the bed and open it. Then she would take out each of the qualities and gifts that she needed for the following day. She would see herself dress, makeup, and unpack her notes.

She would then see herself walking from her room to the conference room. As she approached the podium, she would be bathed in the goodwill of the audience who would be eagerly awaiting her delivery. She would stand for a moment and compose herself and she would glance around the room, encountering happy anticipation in the faces of her fellow bankers. Quickly she would see herself turning the pages of her notebook and reading the list of her qualities and gifts. She would then run through her presentation and at the end would be greeted with warm approbation and applause. The most enthusiastic clapping would be that of her immediate superior.

Annabel is now very successful indeed,

and the greater part of her job is making presentations. Her boss has gone to the banking equivalent of broken biscuits! Annabel combined relaxation, visualisation and affirmations to turn her weakest area into her greatest strength.

LATCH ON TO THE AFFIRMATIVE

Hope... is the companion of power, and the mother of success; for who so hopes has within him the gift of miracles.

SAMUEL SMILES

ELIMINATE THE NEGATIVE

What are affirmations? They are statements of faith and belief that you repeat to yourself with emotional intensity, for the purpose of creating a specific reality in your life. They can be used to transform the faintest hope, the intangible impulse of thought, into tangible reality. The important thing is to identify what it is that you want to achieve. You must set some realistic goals for yourself, and re-educate your subconscious to correct the imbalance that negative conditioning has created. Affirmation is the power of words used in a meditative state of mind to replace a negative self–image and low expectations with a positive view of yourself and high expectations, in any given situation. I suppose they are a kind of self-hypnosis. Most people will have heard of the famous affirmation 'Every day, in every way, I am getting better and better', created I believe, by Dale Carnegie. In a way this is the perfect affirmation to begin with, as it contains all that is positive. It is very, very important if affirmations are to work to leave no room for doubt in their expression.

AFFIRMATIONS

In the pages that follow, I give many examples of possible affirmations for specific situations, but it is often those that you compose for yourself that are most effective. I must repeat that the most important aspect of this technique is to believe utterly in your ability to succeed. I have mentioned the necessity to set realistic goals for yourself. By this I mean, do not make four long lists of aspects of your life or personality that you would like to change or achieve tomorrow. This sort of unrealistic goal-setting leads only to failure and discouragement. However it may be that you will need to change more than one set of beliefs simultaneously if you are to achieve success. The truth is that creating outstanding results often requires extensive reconditioning. Most people find it difficult to change even a single core belief consistently, much less changing several. Unless you find a way to change multiple beliefs simultaneously, you are likely to continue being frustrated in your efforts to achieve your goals.

The most certain way to succeed is to use some of the methods of self-discovery that we have discussed, in order to establish the changes that you would like to make. By now you will be expert at relaxation and visualisation and possibly dream working. Now it is time to combine those techniques with a little honest introspection. Do not be hard on yourself, this exercise is not about knocking yourself down in order to build yourself up again. Just take time to consider what it is you would most like to change. It could be that you would like to be more successful at work; more respected by your colleagues and superiors. It might be that you would like to make friends easily and be confident in social situations. It may well be that you would love to make your needs better understood in close personal relationships or to change your attitude to wealth. It could be that you want to lose or gain weight; or give up smoking, gambling or an addiction to shopping. The happy news is that whatever your goals the techniques for success are exactly the same. Relax, visualise and repeat your chosen affirmations to make quite sure that

your subconscious gets the message.
The other good news is that you can
and should start right this minute.

You don't have to waste a second:
pick a short-term goal and begin now.
Tell yourself that you will repeat a
one-word simple affirmation, ten
times with the next hour and do it.
Try 'Smile' for example, or 'Calm'. You
could try a short sentence: 'I am
successful' is a good start.
Don't agonize, think it; believe it; say
it! Do it now!

STEPS TO SUCCESS
*Immediate action creates and sustains momentum. Do not base your choice on whether or not you already believe the affirmation or if the belief seems possible to you at this moment. Repeating affirmations with emotional intensity and a feeling of certainty will eventually instil the beliefs in your subconscious mind.

*Write the affirmation at least ten to twenty times a day. For best results, write it down ten to twenty times as soon as you wake up and ten to twenty times before you go to bed. This allows you to set your direction before the day starts and plant the seed in your subconscious mind before you go to sleep. You must be consistent. It is strange but you will begin to find that the affirmation pops unbidden into your mind at odd times. You will also begin to notice the affirmations shaping your other thoughts throughout the course of the day. As the affirmations create more and more similar thoughts, you will create a direction and build momentum towards your goal. It's a kind of snowball effect.

*Stand in front of the mirror before you shave or brush your teeth and repeat your affirmation out loud. Yes, you will feel silly at first, but repeating your affirmation out loud at least five to ten times reinforces your written affirmation. This may sound like a lot of work but just remember it has taken a lifetime to instil negative thoughts into your subconscious; it takes real perseverance to reverse the process. It is very important to repeatedly write and speak your affirmations out loud for maximum effect.

*As you write and speak your affirmations, feel their emotional power in your body. If you act like a star you will be treated like one! Visualise yourself as having already created this result in your life. Feel the way you would feel if you already had these qualities and desires fulfilled. Hear the things you will hear when this affirmation becomes an everyday reality. Breathe the way you would breathe if this affirmation were already true. Move your body as if this were already a conditioned belief. Does this type of conditioning take time and effort? Absolutely...on a daily basis. There is no quick solution. You must follow through with these steps every day for a long period of time. You may have been inspired for a few days, as one is when one starts a diet or new health regime. Then, after the motivational 'high' wears off, you fall back into old patterns of behaviour. Or you get so busy that it is easier to 'forget' your affirmations. Try to be consistent and feel the power grow.

In the following pages you will find several suggestions for affirmations in particular contexts. Space does not allow me to create visualisations for all the affirmations listed, but I hope that the examples I give will serve to illustrate the power of affirmations and offer some guidelines for creating your own. As we said at the start, it is *your* life and by definition your goals are intensely personal and only you can make them happen. Use your imagination, and change your life.

§

I AM AN 'A' STUDENT

One of the most stressful experiences which many of us share, and sadly, very early in life, is that of examinations and the pressure to perform well in them. Nowadays, so much seems to depend on the passing of each phase of interviews and exams, in order to be able to pursue our chosen goals. Unfortunately, in their attempts to encourage, prepare and cajole students into doing well, parents and teachers very often increase rather than diminish the inevitable pressure that young people suffer. Sometimes either the student or his parents have unreasonable expectations. Maybe the family has a tradition of going into the law or medicine, but their son or daughter has artistic talent and little aptitude for science or adversarial casework and yet is being encouraged to aim for a university course that is unsuited to her capabilities. Perhaps a student is very keen not to disappoint his or her parents and teachers, and expects too much from himself. Sometimes adults undermine the confidence of students, quite unintentionally, by using sarcasm or criticism to spur them on to greater achievements. Young people often take admonishments that they are slow or lazy, untidy or simply not like an older sibling, very much to heart. It is also quite possible to revise too hard and to go to pieces at the last moment, overwhelmed by the momentous occasion. Any or all of these can impair performance on the day. There are three golden rules for using your power in these circumstances.

～

*The first is to consider your choices about which course to follow very carefully in the first instance. It may take a great deal of rational discussion with those who care about you and your future to find exactly the right course for you. Be open to the wisdom and experience of your elders, but try to be clear about your own needs and goals. Research available courses carefully and be prepared to put your case calmly and honestly, if you expect any opposition to your plans.

*Once you have agreed upon a course

of action, prepare properly. I realize that sounds very boring but no amount of positive thinking will help if you haven't studied the texts, learnt the formulae and read around the subject. Try to get as much practice as you can in answering questions under examination conditions too. The basic building blocks do need to be in place!

*As examinations draw near, make sure you get plenty of rest and fresh air and do remember to eat properly. Then, with your goals firmly in mind, prepare yourself for the process of revision and the examination itself. This is where affirmations and visualisation can be most beneficial.

§

REVISION

Now is a good moment to review the preparation we can make to build a bridge between our conscious and subconscious minds. I imagine that you will have prepared a timetable for your revision. Now is the time to build in ten to fifteen minutes before each session for relaxation and perhaps meditation. Take ten minutes to prepare a list of short affirmations to repeat to yourself after your meditation. The following are just suggestions; you may find it easiest to tailor your own, to suit the subject and personal style of your revision.

AFFIRMATIONS FOR REVISION

I am an intelligent and diligent student.

Learning comes easily to me.

I have a very good memory.

Facts come readily to mind whenever
I need them.

I find it easy to concentrate when I am
studying.

I am not distracted from my good
intentions.

I will remember everything that I learn
today.

I manage my time well and I am confident of success.

I am relaxed and confident in everything I attempt.

I am confident of success.

Sit comfortably and quietly where you won't be disturbed. The tip of your nose should be in line with your navel, arms relaxed by your sides. Take some deep breaths. When time is at a premium, you may prefer to do a simple breathing meditation (see page 30.) If you have been practising regularly, choose your favourite technique. Focus all your attention on your breathing and try to keep your mind clear. Visualise yourself in the act of revising. You are calm and relaxed and your concentration is complete. The material is familiar and you are confident that your brain is absorbing it. Repeat each of your chosen affirmations five times. Then slowly open your eyes and begin work, You should feel both refreshed and energized.

Many people find it useful to write their affirmations down on removable sticky notes and put them where they can see them during their revision sessions. It can be very useful, if you find such things an aid to memory, to choose a particular place to revise each subject and to put a different object for each subject, each alien to the environment, within your line of vision. This object will then become associated in your unconscious mind with the matter under study. A flower, or a feather for example, or a crystal can all work well. With practice you will find it easy to see this object in your mind's eye whenever you want to remember a particular piece of information, and during the exam itself this short cut to memory can be very useful indeed. Other people find a scented candle or aromatherapy oil burner, or stick of incense can act as a catalyst to memory. Again choose a different aroma for each session. Do keep candles and oil burners away from books and papers though and never leave them burning unattended. A piece of music can be used to the same good effect.

Another tried and tested aid can be used as you commit information to memory. Take yourself on an imaginary journey around the house and place the things you need to remember in particular rooms. Hamlet's soliloquy in the bathroom for example, imagine him proclaiming in the shower. When you need to retrieve the information you simply make the journey again collecting your knowledge along the way.

§

PREPARATION FOR THE EXAMINATION
The Night before:

Compose a list of five affirmations, or use those suggested here. Sometimes one-word affirmations are enough, and I offer a few suggestions below. You will need to repeat these to yourself, with complete faith in their success, at least five times each.

ONE-WORD AFFIRMATIONS

Calm
Confident
Clear-headed
Focused
Energized
Successful
Fulfilled
Triumphant
Relaxed

When you are confident that you have made all preparations – you have checked the time and place of the exam, and have the correct equipment and have set the alarm if necessary – take ten minutes for relaxation. Once again use your favourite technique. When your mind is clear and focused, visualise yourself entering the examination room. You are calm and confident; you are looking forward to demonstrating your knowledge; you know that there is plenty of time. See yourself sitting and reading the questions through calmly; you smile as you realize that they present no difficulties. Next you see yourself writing confidently. Finally you have completed the paper and laid down your pen; see yourself smile and silently congratulate yourself on good work, well done.

On the day:
The occasion itself and the solemn atmosphere surrounding it can create such a level of anxiety that we are afraid that we won't do ourselves justice in the examination itself. We are often deprived of the comforts with which we associate work. Perhaps you like a particular spot in which to study or a special piece of music to be playing whilst you work. Perhaps you need complete solitude or maybe you can only work in a busy library where you can look up from time to time and consider what other people are doing and saying. Maybe you like to nibble on a biscuit or sip a cup of tea or

coffee. In an examination situation we are deprived of all this. This is where your visualisation can be so useful. If you have used some of the techniques above to help instil information into your subconscious you can use your visualisation skills to recall them.

As you sit in the examination room, take a moment to close your eyes. Take a deep breath and settle your breathing into a regular pattern. Use your mediation experience to recall the exact circumstances in which you committed the information you need to memory. Repeat your chosen affirmations or use those listed, to yourself one last time. Congratulations! You deserve to succeed and you will!

AFFIRMATIONS FOR SUCCESS

I am calm and in control.

I remember my revision notes clearly.

I am breathing evenly.

My mind is clear and alert.

I read and absorb the questions.

I am confident that all my hard work will be rewarded.

I understand the questions and I am able to consider what the examiners are looking for.

I am prepared and will have no difficulty accessing the right information.

I am doing my best and that IS good enough.

I can take a few minutes to organize my thoughts.

I am successful and move on towards my goals.

THE DATING GAME

We all want to meet and fall in love with one special person and live happily ever after. Sadly, this is another of the circumstances in which early experiences of rejection can destroy our confidence in our own essential right to be loved. Many young children believe themselves to be responsible for the break-up of their parents' marriages, or the unhappiness of siblings. Since our survival as small children depends on our self-centredness, sometimes we cannot distinguish between the things that are our responsibility and those that are not. Taking inappropriate responsibility for the unhappiness of others is very common. We are responsible *to* others to act with integrity and care but we are only responsible *for* those who are truly dependent on us for their survival.

Children are never responsible for adults or their happiness. Yet, many children believe that daddy would be home more often if they were only more lovable, or mummy wouldn't cry if only they had drunk all their milk and put their toys away. Adults often reinforce this feeling with hasty words like 'Now look what you've done, Mummy's got a headache.' Tragically some children are the victims of abuse or deliberate cruelty and need professional help to recover their self-respect and confidence. But even in the normal course of events, parents are sometimes guilty of threatening to withhold love and affection as a means of behavioural control. The net result is that few of us grow up without dents in our self-image as lovable human beings. Never is this more evident than when we hope to meet our potential life partner at a party or perhaps have got as far as a first date. Now is the perfect opportunity to offer our egos up for a battering and to persuade our would-be partner that they have made a mistake; we are not the attractive, interesting person they thought us. Using your visualisation and affirmation skills it is possible to break bad habits of self-denigration and present ourselves as we truly are, warm, lovable, good company and open to the joy of a fulfilling relationship.

You know the drill by now. When an exciting opportunity comes along, we get an adrenaline rush that can be controlled and directed as happy excitement and anticipation or fills us with abject terror. So the first thing to do is to relax using our deep breathing techniques. Then as you prepare for your date or party, take ten minutes to practise the following affirmations, whilst you visualise a wonderful evening. You meet the man or woman of your dreams. They smile at you and you return their smile openly and warmly. You talk and listen carefully, giving them the opportunity to tell you about themselves. They listen attentively to you as you establish all that you have in common. The whole occasion is one of pleasure and joy.

You return home eager to see one
another again.

Don't forget to invite me to the
wedding!

AFFIRMATIONS FOR DATING

I am beautiful.

I have a right to love and be loved.

I am attractive and lovable.

I listen to others and I am interested in their lives.

I smile and look others in the eye.

I am calm and in control.

I am able to consider my own needs.

I am responsible for my own happiness.

I am not afraid to take a risk in this relationship.

I am free to choose the level of my own involvement in this relationship.

I can make my own needs known.

I am attentive to my partner's needs.

I am not responsible for his or her complete happiness and I do not expect too much from others.

I am able to be honest and truthful.

I am true to myself.

I am independent and free.

I am interested and interesting

I am warm and loving

ONE-WORD AFFIRMATIONS

One of the most important rules of successful personal empowerment is to identify your goal, and then take at least one positive step towards achieving it. This is one of the benefits of one-word affirmations. For example, the next time you are in a meeting and find yourself thinking 'I wish my boss would listen to my suggestions for once', do something immediately. Repeat the word 'positive' in your head five or six times. As you do so visualise yourself gaining his or her attention and putting your point of view. Feel as you will feel when he congratulates you on your good idea, and you have the approbation and gratitude of your colleagues. You may not have an immediate opportunity to realize this goal, but add it to your list, repeat the affirmation and visualisation throughout the day and you will be surprised to find that at the next available opportunity this affirmation could become a reality. Don't be put off by the fact that results might not be immediate, the important thing is to keep the momentum going.

One-word affirmations are power words that you can repeat with emotional intensity and certainty to direct your thoughts towards the achievement of your desires. They have some advantages over more complex conceptual affirmations, as they are quick and easy to remember. They do not present such a challenge to your deeply held belief system as their more powerful cousins. If you repeat the affirmation 'I am slender and willowy and I look great in clothes' your conscious mind and indeed your waistline will immediately run interference by refusing to accept that this is true. In time it can become true, because you will be supporting your body's efforts with your mind's determination, but at the moment when you recognize that you would like it to be so, you will have more success in keeping your affirmation simple. 'Elegant' or 'Light' might be good words to start with here. Focusing on one word gives your subconscious a chance to become accustomed to the idea of a slender you, especially if you reinforce this with a visualisation of the slim and willowy you of your imagination. Once the seed is sown you can move on to more advanced affirmations. The convenience of one-word affirmations also overcomes the excuse that all this positive thinking is too time-consuming. You can use them several times a day while you are doing other things, For example, while you are driving, while you are getting ready in the morning, as you drift off to sleep etc. They are also great daily reinforcement of more complex affirmations and will often just pop into your head when you are faced with a situation that challenges the new positive you.

~

For example, perhaps you find a daily commute to work in traffic very stressful, and you are fighting this with a programme of relaxation affirmations. One morning the traffic snarl-up is so bad that you are going to be seriously late for work. The word 'relax' or 'peace' may well pop into your head unbidden, and stop you tipping over the edge into road rage. I have been surprised to find that this actually happens.

The choice of affirmations is entirely yours and I strongly recommend creating your own. I have found that for one-word affirmations, choosing a primary word from a longer affirmation that I am using regularly works well, as they work together to strengthen the power of both.

The following selection is designed to start you off and I must acknowledge Power Affirmations™ at www.poweraffirmations.com for much inspiration and for generously allowing many of the following to swell my affirmation vocabulary. Their creator is also convinced that affirmations are more effective when they are heard as well as spoken. It is possible to record your affirmations on to an audiocassette, and I should mention that many of the lists below and others are available on CD from the website above.

Please remember that your programme

of reconditioning will be one hundred percent more effective if you practise the relaxation and visualisation exercises in the earlier part of this book in conjunction with the more life-changing goal lists.

∾

ONE WORD AFFIRMATIONS

Abundance
    Electric
        Knowledge
            Relaxed
Acceptance
    Energy
        Lavish
            Release
Accumulate
    Enthusiasm
        Lead
            Remember
Advance
    Eternal
        Life
            Renewed

Answer
       Excellence
              Listen
                      Repetition
Authority
       Excess
              Loving
                      Respect
Beauty
       Expect
              Loyal
                      Responsible
Belief
       Faith
              Luxury
                      Result
Benefit
       Family
              Massive
                      Sales

Blessings
       Genius
              Meditate
                    Seed
Bountiful
       Gift
              Mercy
                    Silence
Calm
       Give
              Now
                    Solved
Cancel
       Great
              Open
                    Spontaneous
Cause
       Grow
              Outstanding
                    Strength

Certainty
      Guidance
            Peaceful
                  Subconscious
Circulate
      Habit
            Perfect
                  Success
Compassion
      Happy
            Pleasure
                  Surplus
Complete
      Harmony
            Possible
                  Thankful
Confidence
      Harvest
            Power
                  Think

Connected
　　Healing
　　　　Praise
　　　　　　Thoughtful
Consistent
　　Health
　　　　Promotion
　　　　　　Together
Courage
　　Idea
　　　　Purpose
　　　　　　Touch
Create
　　Imagine
　　　　Quality
　　　　　　Transform
Decision
　　Income
　　　　Quickly
　　　　　　Trustworthy

Delighted
        Infinite
                Quiet
                        Truth
Desire
        Intelligent
                Reason
                        Vision
Destiny
        Intuition
                Receive
                        Wealth
Dream
        Invisible
                Recreation
                        Wisdom
Effect
        Joy
                Rejoice
                        Wonderful

AFFIRMATIONS FOR A NEW SELF-IMAGE

I am now filled with faith, certainty and confidence. I now feel these emotions in my body.

I am now confident and assertive.

I now walk and move with assurance, poise and personal power.

I am now a powerful and charismatic personality.

I am growing more and more attractive everyday.

My confidence and competence are exploding massively everyday.

I am now friendly, outgoing and confident.

I am now bold and courageous. I now seize my opportunities immediately.

I now have the ability to change anything in my life that I choose to change. I take complete responsibility for my life.

When I speak to others, I look them straight in the eye and speak with confidence knowing that I am equal to every person I meet regardless of their social status or accomplishments.

I can now create a state of total certainty and confidence at a moment's notice, anytime I need it.

I now move my body with poise and confidence.

Every time I close my eyes and breathe deeply, my confidence expands and fills my whole being.

I now see myself as exactly the person I want to be confident, self-assured, healthy and prosperous.

I now hold other people and myself in high esteem.

Everyday in every way I am growing more and more confident.

My confident energy, enthusiasm and passion are increasing massively everyday.

Because I am committed to constant and never ending improvement, my performance is improving everyday.

What I imagine I can do, I can do.

∾

AFFIRMATIONS FOR CONFIDENCE

I am now fearless, courageous and bold.

I receive wisdom and knowledge from my subconscious mind every moment of my life.

I apply my faith with consistent acts of courage.

The expression on my face now communicates certainty and confidence.

I am now a highly charismatic and powerful person.

I now inspire and expand my imagination with enthusiasm.

I now relive the most joyous moments of my life. And these moments inspire me to greater confidence and a greater feeling of self-worth.

I act as if I already have all the confidence I need and desire.

I speak to others and myself with confidence, certainty and conviction.

My thoughts, presence, charm and charisma now inspire others to greater self-confidence and personal power.

I now radiate confidence and certainty in the presence of other people.

When I speak, the tone of my voice communicates strength, courage and confidence.

I am now confident, assertive and decisive in every situation.

I now create outstanding confidence by repeatedly rehearsing in my mind and imagining the results I want in advance.

I am now an outstanding leader who leads with confidence.

I increase my self-confidence by increasing my skills and abilities everyday.

As I rehearse the results I want in my thoughts before they happen, my skill and confidence expand massively.

Other people find me to be a fascinating and interesting person.

∾

AFFIRMATIONS FOR ACHIEVING GOALS

I now put my body into a peak state of absolute certainty knowing that I can create any positive result to which I am committed.

I am now living a life of design rather than a life of reaction.

I am now absolutely clear about the specific results I want in every area of my life.

I now make my future my present. My future is now.

I now celebrate the achievement of my goals before they occur in the physical world.

Whenever I set a definite goal, I take immediate action towards its attainment to create and sustain massive momentum.

I am now spending my time, energy, and emotion on the goals that are most important to me rather than responding to the demands of other people.

I am in control.

Urgency is not my friend. Through results-focused planning and delegating to others, I minimize the amount of time I spend addressing the urgent demands of other people.

I now do only what I do best and get other people to do the rest.

I now delegate tasks that do not require my direct attention and focus to other people.

My subconscious mind now provides me with the specific massive action plans I need to attain my desired results.

∾

My subconscious mind is now consistently presenting me with updated plans to achieve my goals even when I am playing, eating or sleeping.

I now carefully measure and manage my progress towards my desired results everyday.

I am now highly flexible. I carefully monitor the results that I am getting and quickly adjust my actions until I receive the specific results I desire.

I accelerate my progress towards my desired results by studying other people who have been outstanding in that area.

Using tapes books, music and anything else around me that is easily accessible, I now create a controlled environment that keeps my mind focused on my primary outcomes everyday.

I do not adapt to my environment. I persist in making my environment adapt to me.

I am now focused on the results I want, driven by a passionate purpose and charted with massive action plans.

I now see things exactly the way they are, exactly the way I want them, and now take massive action to close that gap.

I now prepare a results-oriented daily plan every evening for the following day.

I feed my momentum monster everyday by consistently taking results-focused action.

When I reach a definite decision, I commit and resolve to the achievement of the end result I desire.

I now create magic moments for family friends and myself.

I now celebrate my achievements in advance.

AFFIRMATIONS FOR HEALTH AND VITALITY

My health, energy and vitality are increasing everyday.

I am a lean, mean, fat-burning, muscle-building machine.

I am growing more and more attractive everyday.

Divine life now flows through every cell in my body.

I now eat all the right foods for optimum health, energy, and peak performance.

My body is healing and regenerating itself everyday.

With every deep breath I take, my body is burning fat and creating massive energy, health and vitality.

My body burns fat regardless of what I eat.

I now see myself filled with health, energy and enthusiasm.

I now have all the energy I need.

I create good health habits quickly and easily.

My body now eliminates all toxins quickly, easily and healthfully.

I am now relaxed and filled with peace of mind. In my relaxed state, my body repairs and heals itself quickly.

All of the cells in my body exist in harmony and peace with every other cell in my body.

❧

I get a full night's rest everyday.
When I sleep, my mind is at peace and the healing powers within my body are magnified.

The creative intelligence that made my body is now transforming every cell according to nature's perfect pattern.

My healing thoughts are now going deep into my subconscious mind and bringing total and continuous healing to my body.

I now enjoy a large variety of water-rich foods that fully cleanse and nourish every cell in my body.

I sleep in peace and I wake in joy.

Through peaceful sleep, my body and mind are renewed and restored to perfect health.

❧

AFFIRMATIONS FOR WEALTH

I am now wealthy.

I deserve to be wealthy.

I am now a financial genius.

I am now highly pleasing to myself in the presence of other people.

I now save, spend and invest my money wisely.

My wealth is increasing massively everyday.

I now give away massive amounts of wealth to causes that I believe in.

All the investments I own are profitable.

Every pound I spend returns to me massively multiplied.

I manage my money effectively with precision.

I now have all the money that I want and need.

I now give away large amounts of wealth wisely and intelligently.

I am now creating all of the wealth that I want and need.

My imagination is now creating all the financial abundance that I desire.

The more of my wealth that I give away
wisely, the more my personal wealth
explodes massively.

I now seize my opportunities boldly
and courageously, decisively applying
my faith through my actions.

My imagination now creates all the
wealth I desire.

Through my power of intention, I
effortlessly attract all the wealth I need
and desire.

I habitually give more than I get. I
cheerfully go the extra mile in every
task I undertake.

I am now accumulating vast amounts of wealth consistent with my integrity and honesty.

I respectfully accept the gifts of others with the knowledge that these gifts were intended to gratify the giver more than the receiver.

I am now receptive to unexpected gifts of wealth.

I am a gracious giver and receiver. When I think wealthy thoughts, I become wealthier in all aspects of my life.

My wealth is now multiplying and creating more wealth easily and effortlessly.

My financial abundance is now exploding massively 24 hours a day even when I am playing, eating and sleeping.

An ocean of wealth now surrounds me and I draw from this ocean all I need.

My job is my personal pipeline from which I tap the infinite wealth from my world economy for my personal desires.

I am now earning massive amounts of wealth doing what I love to do while rendering useful service to other people.

Through the power of my subconscious mind, I effortlessly attract all the wealth I need and desire.

I am a money magnet.

Money is forever circulating in my life and there is always a surplus.

I have a responsibility to accumulate vast sums of wealth through useful service to others and to give it back to society through gifts that benefit the entire community.

AFFIRMATIONS FOR FRIENDSHIP

I now make good friends quickly and easily.

Good people are attracted to me every day. They want to meet me.

I now put other people at ease quickly and easily.

I now hold other people and myself in high esteem.

I now surround myself with positive, proactive people.

I always create harmony with others through co-operative effort.

I will succeed by attracting to myself the co-operation of other people.

I will encourage others to help me because of my willingness to help other people.

I will cause other people to believe in me because I believe in them and in myself.

I listen attentively to what others say without interrupting them.

I create synergistic, positive relationships that are fair, honest and healthy.

All my facial expressions are now pleasant and pleasing to other people and myself.

When I greet people, I greet them with gladness in my being.

I now have a magnetic, warm handshake.

When people first meet me, they like me instantly.

I now accomplish my goals with the benefits to others in mind.

I listen to others carefully before responding.

I now develop co-operative alliances with others towards definite, specific objectives quickly and easily.

I now have a keen understanding of myself and of other people.

I treat every person I meet with respect, mercy, tolerance and understanding.

I now look for the good in every person I meet and I find it.

I inspire and empower others to greatness.

I now have favour in the eyes of every person I meet.

I now have a highly pleasing personality.

All of my contacts with other people are smooth and pleasant.

I express my honest and sincere appreciation and praise for others easily and often.

I arouse a feeling of enthusiasm for good things in other people.

When speaking with others, I attempt to look at things through their point of view as well as my own.

I am now genuinely interested in other people.

I wear a sincere, heart-warming smile everywhere I go. My genuine smile comes from deep within my innermost being.

I remember the names of other people easily and effortlessly.

I encourage other people to talk about themselves and I listen intently.
When I speak to others, I focus on their interests not mine.

When I need someone to do something, I make him or her feel happy to do it by pointing out the benefits to them.

I sincerely recognize the value in every person I meet and make a genuine effort to make them feel important.

AFFIRMATIONS TO GIVE UP SMOKING

I am not dependent on anything.

I have no desire to smoke.

My lungs are clean and clear.

I enter a room with confidence.

My smile is bright and my breath fresh.

I am uninfluenced by others smoking.

I am confident that I have given up smoking for life.

I can have a drink or coffee after a meal without thinking about a cigarette.

I do not need to replace one bad habit with another.

My appetite is completely under control.

I am calm and cheerful.

I can face any situation with confidence.

I have more money to spend on harmless pleasure.

I will live longer and be healthy.

I am sweet-tempered and calm.

AFFIRMATIONS FOR WEIGHT LOSS

I am slender and willowy.

My body burns fat effortlessly.

I enjoy fresh fruit and vegetables.

I am not hungry for sweets and sugary foods.

I look great both naked and in my clothes.

I am fitter and healthier.

I sleep well and wake refreshed.

I look terrific in a swimsuit.

I enjoy exercise.

I can run for the bus without getting breathless.

I am attractive and fun to be with.

I am confident and happy.

The fridge holds no terrors for me.

I enjoy water-rich foods that release the toxins from my system.

I drink at least eight glasses of water a day.

I would rather have a piece of fruit than a sticky bun.

AFFIRMATIONS FOR SUCCESS AT WORK

I am worthy of my salary.

I deserve success.

I have good ideas and express them well.

When I speak, I do so confidently and clearly.

I am a valued staff member.

I acknowledge the contribution of others and remember to thank them.

I am always appreciative of any help and support I receive.

I help and support others.

I am a good team member.

I have qualities of leadership that I use without favour.

I am not afraid of competition.

When one idea doesn't work I always have another.

I am punctual and diligent.

My colleagues like and trust me.

I know how to prioritise my work.

I never expect others to do what I would not do myself.

I am successful and confident.

My job is fulfilling because I make it so.

My superiors like and appreciate me.

~